Contents

A MACDONALD BOOK

© Hachette, Paris, 1986

First published in France in 1986 by
Hachette Jeunesse
as *Animaux des Maisons et des Jardins*

First published in Great Britain in 1987 by
Macdonald & Company (Publishers) Ltd
London & Sydney
A BPCC plc company

All rights reserved

Printed and bound in France

Macdonald & Company (Publishers) Ltd
Greater London House
Hampstead Road
London NW1 7QX

Credits
This edition produced for Macdonald Publishers by
Lionheart Books,
10 Chelmsford Square, London NW10 3AR.

Translated by Madeleine Bender
Adapted by Lionel Bender
Artwork services by Radius

British Library Cataloguing in Publication Data
Bender, Lionel
    Homes and gardens.—(Nature notes; 2)
    1. Garden fauna—Europe—Juvenile
    literature 2. Household ecology—Europe
    —Juvenile literature
    I. Title II. Bender, Madeleine III. Series
    591.94   QL253

ISBN 0-356-11991-2

HOMES AND GARDENS

Translated by Madeleine Bender
Adapted by Lionel Bender

How many people who live in flats or apartment blocks have often dreamt of living in a house surrounded by a garden? Small and plain as a garden might be, compared to a world of concrete and asphalt it is an island of greenery, a protected space, a territory where animals and plants can find refuge.

Many animals are attracted by plants or ponds that you have arranged in the garden to make it a prettier place. Some of these come into the house and make their home there, as do pets. There are among them a few undesirable or unwelcome creatures.

For the gardener or any person living in a house, crushing spiders, worms, flies and snails, and killing moles and mice are common practices. After all, these animals are pests, aren't they? But beware the temptation to get rid of any creature that wants to share your territory. You will find through your experiments and observations that not all of them are pests. The ladybird, the tit and the swallow are useful animals and ones pleasant to watch. They deserve your attention and protection. As for the cat of the house, while it needs a lot of care and attention, it can provide a warm and long-lasting friendship.

Come down to the garden now to observe this little world.

The House Mouse

MRS HOUSE MOUSE

Discreet and shy, the house mouse lives in meadows and woods but is keen to make its home in houses. Here it occupies all the rooms, from cellar to loft, from kitchen to bedrooms.

The mouse's coat varies in colour from grey to brown depending on where it lives. Individuals living in houses usually have a grey coat, those outdoors a brown one. Its long thin tail trails behind it. Its thin pointed muzzle bristles with whiskers. It has small, dark eyes. The mouse cannot see very well but its senses of hearing and smell are highly developed.

Having settled in the house, the mouse feeds on whatever it can find. It is said to be commensal with people as it shares the same food. It does not hoard food and prefers to come out at night to forage. It has no difficulty establishing what can make a suitable meal, and nibbles bags, boxes and all manner of foods.

Mice breed fast. The female is pregnant with its young for about three weeks. The babies are born blind and naked. The mother suckles them for about a month. At the age of between eight and ten weeks the young are, in turn, able to breed. In the wild, from spring to autumn, a mouse can have from four to eight litters depending on the quantity of food available and the weather conditions. In houses, it can breed all the year round.

The house mouse lives in colonies within which individuals feed, rest and hide together and also groom each other. But in a colony each family has its own nest, which is kept separate from the neighbouring ones. Sometimes the

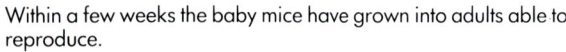

Within a few weeks the baby mice have grown into adults able to reproduce.

The mouse has typical rodent incisors – long, curved, chisel-edged, continuously growing.

house mouse can be a different colour from its usual grey-brown. The white mouse is in fact an albino house mouse.

IS THERE A MOUSE IN THE HOUSE?

The mouse leaves marks of its passage throughout the house. Around the nibbled potatoes you will find small, dark, usually long and thin, droppings.

To find its way back to its food in the dark, the mouse marks a path to the place with scent. You can soon recognize this distinctive smell when you open the cupboard or larder. Or maybe the cat will bring the mouse to you on returning from one of its hunting trips. You might just catch a glimpse of

the mouse as it tries to get back to its hole, racing across the room in the twinkling of an eye.

IF THERE IS ONE, CAN YOU STUDY IT?

It is difficult to study the mouse's lifestyle in the home as the animal ventures out only at night. As it is timid, it does not appear until everything is quiet. You can try to find the paths it follows in your house.

In the places you think it often visits, place some sheets of cardboard covered with fine sand. When the mouse walks over one of these track-traps it will leave its footprints on it. Place scraps of food for it in a saucer on the floor – some cheese rind or pieces of potato, for example. If the mouse has been attracted, it will have walked across the cardboard and, the next morning, you will be able to see its tracks – small thin pawmarks, barely showing on either side of a line left by the tail.

A HIGH-PITCHED SQUEAK

Another clue to the mouse's presence is the sound of tiny squeaks. It has recently been discovered that mice and other small rodents use high-pitched sounds, or ultrasonics, to communicate with one another. A mouse's ears are more sensitive to such sounds than ours so we can hear only a part of their 'conversation'. If you know there are mice living behind the skirting board put one ear to the wall and listen carefully. You may hear their squeaks.

YOU MUST GET RID OF IT

Even if it is fun to observe the house mouse, there always comes a time when you have to get rid of it. It will nibble the groceries and gnaw the furnishings, papers and books to line its nest. One nesting mouse will turn, in a few months, into an army, as these small rodents reproduce at a surprising speed.

To have a cat in the house is a very effective way of keeping away mice, which it catches, eats, takes to its young or abandons at your feet. Some people prefer to use poison. However, this method can endanger cats, dogs, and other pets, which might eat the poisoned mouse. The mousetrap, with a spring held by thin wire and baited with some food, remains the simplest and best device to protect the house even if it seems rather cruel.

The Edible Brown Snail

A SHELL AND HORNS

Along the garden path crawls a snail. Its brown shell rocks on its back. The animal appears to be feeling its way around with its 'horns', which are in fact tentacles. It has four of these: the two longer ones, at the top, each end in a dark spot, an eye, and the two shorter ones, at the bottom, feel the ground. The crescent-shaped mouth is below the tentacles.

When the snail is moving, it is its head and 'foot' that you see, touching the ground. The rest of its body is hidden in its shell. If you touch the snail it will disappear completely inside the shell. This is how it protects itself from its enemies – birds and hedgehogs in particular – but also from harmful weather conditions such as heat, cold and dryness.

Like earthworms, snails are hermaphrodites, that is they have both male and female organs. However, two of them have to pair up to breed. They mate during the warm damp days of the months of May and June, keeping their bodies pressed closely together for several hours.

They lay their eggs in the ground throughout the summer. About four weeks after the eggs are laid in this humid environment, baby snails are born with thin and transparent shells. They measure only about half a centimetre in length.

The snail feeds only on plants. In gardens it particularly likes lettuces, cabbages and carrot leaves. It eats by shredding the food with its tongue, called the radula. If you listen carefully, you can sometimes hear a squeaking noise as it eats a leaf.

A DAMP ENVIRONMENT

Snails like dampness so they come out in large numbers as soon as it rains. Then you can see them almost everywhere – in the vegetable garden, on the walls of the houses, on paths.

The rest of the time, snails hide in cool, damp, sheltered spots, for example under nettles, in an old wooden shed or in an empty flowerpot forgotten in the grass.

You can sometimes find a snail coiled inside its shell, the opening sealed by a chalky plug, the epiphragm. The animal shuts itself up in its shell in this way to hibernate and protect itself against too harsh a winter or too dry a summer. To make the snail come out of its 'house', simply sprinkle it with tepid water.

The snail eats by shredding food with its tongue.

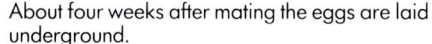

About four weeks after mating the eggs are laid underground.

AT A SNAIL'S PACE

The snail's slowness is famous. It moves at a speed of about five metres an hour. To cross a road, therefore, takes it at least an hour, and its slowness does not allow it to escape from its enemies. Most snails end up crushed by the wheels of a car or eaten.

You can easily observe how the snail moves by placing it on a pane of glass. Look at the snail from the other side. Its foot has ridges that extend from front to back.

A mucus, a sort of slime, that is secreted by a gland under the snail's head allows its foot to glide over surfaces and forms the shiny trail the animal leaves behind.

IMMENSELY STRONG

The snail's foot is a powerful muscle, as you can find out for yourself. With

Breeding jar: humidity must be constant.
1. water inlet   2. air inlet

With continuous wave-like movements of its foot, the snail moves on all surfaces.

some sticky tape, attach the string of a small toy trailer to the animal's shell. Keep loading this vehicle with more and more pebbles for as long as the snail can continue to pull it along. A snail weighing twelve grams has managed to pull a two-kilogram load – about 170 times its own weight. To show the same strength an adult person would have to pull a goods truck!

A DELICACY

In French cuisine, snails are a gourmet delicacy. Picture in your mind people going out to gather some snails as soon as the rain stops and then having a magnificent feast. But take note! Preparing snails for eating is a long process – it takes about two weeks – and often the hundred or so snails that have been gathered for the meal gradually rot and so end up in the dustbin. Most people find it easier to buy ready-prepared frozen or tinned snails.

In some countries there are strict laws governing the gathering of snails and it is even forbidden altogether in certain areas of France and in Switzerland, where the edible snail is in danger of becoming extinct.

In Britain there are several kinds of snail. They differ in their size, shape and the colour of their shell. The garden snail has apparently been eaten since Roman times. The Romans actually cultivated snails in 'cochlearia' or snail farms and recommended eating them to cure coughs and stomach aches.

At the seaside, beneath the seaweed and in rock crevices, a small brown-black snail can be found. It is called the winkle. This small shelled animal, or mollusc, is also edible.

Flies

ANNOYING FLIES

Flies are small, dull-coloured insects, mostly grey. Some, however, have a brightly coloured abdomen. The head is large and has two protruding eyes each made up of many tiny windows or facets; they are called compound eyes.

Flies do not have mouthparts for chewing food but instead possess a tube-like proboscis that works like a straw. They are sucking insects. They only consume foods that are liquid or have been liquefied by their saliva.

Flies are fast flyers. They have just one pair of functional wings, which are transparent and ribbed. Behind the wings are two knobbed organs that are very important as they help the animals keep their balance in flight. These organs are clearly visible in mosquitoes, which are closely related to flies. The insect's buzz or hum is produced by the rapid wingbeat.

Flies are able to walk vertically on walls or upside-down on ceilings just as easily as on the flat. At the tip of their feet are pads covered with oily sticky hairs that enable the insects to walk everywhere, even on such smooth surfaces as glass.

It is usually in rotting matter and excrement that flies lay their several hundred yellowish-white eggs from which the larvae will hatch – the maggots fishermen know so well. All fly larvae feed on the materials on which the adult laid the eggs. The larvae then change into pupae, which have a hard, brown case, the cocoon. To come out of this prison, the young fly makes its blood rush to its head. This swells its brow which bursts the case. It can then fly away and is ready to breed.

RAPID REPRODUCTION

By laying their eggs in dead animals or organic waste, flies take an active part in nature in getting rid of decaying matter – leftovers from the fox's meal, excrement of cows, horses and the like.

The carcass of an animal provides the adult fly with food, gives it a place to lay its eggs and satisfies all the needs of the larvae.

A fly needs less than a day to find a dead animal and lay its eggs in it. A single female can lay as many as 200 eggs at a time. The larvae's growth and development are also very fast. In general, the young fly emerges from the cocoon about twelve days after the eggs have been laid. In particularly warm weather, however, the whole development from egg-laying to adult fly may take only seven days.

The flies that come into the house, however, do not all belong to the same species and they differ in the way they feed and breed, and where they prefer to live. Also they do not all eat the same foods nor lay their eggs on the same materials.

THE HOUSE FLY

The fly that you can see in the spring in your house and which lands on milk drops or in the sugar bowl is the most common species. It leaves its excrement almost everywhere – small black spots on light-bulbs, on the ceiling or on food. It moves about on refuse and decaying matter and can carry microscopic disease-causing organisms on its feet-pads and on its proboscis.

House flies are very numerous. Even if they fly about silently, their presence soon becomes irritating. Half a lemon

bluebottle.

Very quickly, the eggs hatch into the larvae called maggots.

greenbottle.

house fly.

The fly has two large compound eyes and a tube-like mouth that coils up under its head.

studded with cloves is all that is needed to keep them away, so people say.

BLUEBOTTLE, GREENBOTTLE

Another type of fly particularly likes pieces of meat, where it will readily lay its eggs. Larger than the house fly and with its abdomen coloured a magnificent metallic blue, the bluebottle flies in noisy zigzags, crashing into window panes and lamps.

The maggots that fishermen use to bait their hooks are the larvae of the greenbottle, a fly which shimmers green and gold. These maggots have to be kept cool to slow down their change, or metamorphosis, into adult flies. Should they be kept too warm or for too long, the fisherman will have a nasty surprise on opening his bait box. All the larvae will have been replaced by the brown pupae cases from which the young greenbottles will emerge.

The greenbottle particularly likes the excrements of mammals, for example cow-pats and horse-dung.

THE VINEGAR FLY

A small fly has just come into the kitchen. It flies over the fruit bowl and lands on the neck of an open lemonade bottle or jam jar.

It is the little vinegar fly, *Drosophila*, also known as fruit fly. It measures only three or four millimetres in length but is very useful to us. First, it carries the substances that allow wine to ferment. Second, its fast breeding rate and the way in which its physical features such as eye colour, change from one generation to another have led to a better understanding of how the cells in the human body work.

The Great Tit

A FAMILIAR ACROBAT

A common sight in our garden, the great tit is easy to recognize. Its head is black and has white cheeks. Black feathers also cover its neck and continue in a line down the middle of its chest, which is yellow. Its back is grey-green.

The beak is black, thin, but powerful enough to allow the tit to eat foods other than insects and spiders when these become scarce in winter. It then feeds on seeds and berries and, enjoying fatty foods, it will often pierce milk-bottle tops to get the cream.

The great tit nests in natural holes in tree trunks, not very high above the ground, in wall cracks, under roofs, and does not mind occupying old nests. It lines its nest with moss, roots, grass, down and hairs.

In the nest, it lays between eight and thirteen eggs, which are white with rust-coloured spots. The female sits on the eggs for about two weeks. There are often two broods a year, depending on the climate.

The chicks are covered in grey down and display an orange throat that can be clearly seen when they stretch up, mouth wide open, to receive their food. Both parents feed them caterpillars at a non-stop rate; it is estimated that the young eat 8000 of these in the twenty days they spend in the nest!

The great tit and its cousins, the blue tit and the marsh tit, which you can also see in your garden, are acrobats. While looking for food, they move along twigs and the thinnest of branches, and find themselves upside-down swinging in extraordinary positions. Thanks to the firm grasp of their feet, they can cling to bark and flexible stalks.

A RESTAURANT FOR TITS

In winter, the great tit is the most common visitor of feeding tables and bird baths.

In your garden, fix a platform on a post one metre from the ground and place on it a container filled with margarine and sunflower seeds. The tit is bound to discover your offering. If you keep topping up this feeding-table container, the bird will get used to coming to it and will become less and less shy. Then, if you hide well and keep perfectly still and quiet, you will be able to observe the great tit at close quarters.

With a simple camera set-up, you will even be able to take photographs of the bird of which you will be most proud. Use a camera with a cable-release, put it on a tripod, and hide all this behind a screen of branches or cardboard. Give the tit time to get used to this 'hide'. It will soon stop paying attention to it and feel at ease.

AN INDEPENDENT BIRD

When leaving food out for the tit, do not forget that it can quite easily manage without us! It is one of the few birds that can fend for themselves in the winter. It feeds on the few adult insects still around, on larvae, seeds and all sorts of scraps of food that we throw away.

The great tit has a very tough throat and can even eat the pine processionary moth caterpillar, common in much of southern Europe, which most other birds leave alone because of its irritant hairs. However, when winter is too harsh, the ground frozen hard and snow covers everything for a long time, feeding the birds is helpful to them.

Fourteen-day-old chicks. The tit's chicks leave the nest about three weeks after birth.

The tit makes its nest in the holes of old walls.

Some tits will travel several kilometres each day to feed at bird-tables.

When the temperature is below freezing, put out a dish of lukewarm water to quench their thirst. If you change the water often, it will not have enough time to turn to ice.

WHERE TO NEST?

The female great tit chooses its nesting site early in the year, sometimes as early as February. It will only start to line the nest with twigs and small roots at the end of March. It lays its eggs in the nest in April.

The great tit likes to make its home in small, dark places. It will build its nest in the cavities of old walls or in holes in trees but it has no hesitation in picking unusual places, for example letter-boxes, pipes and hollow bricks. It will also occupy old nests that used to belong to other types of bird. This habit, which is peculiar to the great tit, gives you another opportunity to observe it. If you offer it a suitable nesting place, it will gladly occupy it.

WHAT TYPE OF NESTING BOX TO BUILD?

A simple way of making a nesting box for great tits is to take a terracotta flower pot and block the large opening with a piece of wood held in place by wire. Be careful about the size of the hole at the bottom of the pot. It if is too small, blue tits will move into the pot. If it is too big, sparrows will settle in it. The ideal diameter is three centimetres. A small hole can be made larger using an old wood file. All you have to do then is hang up the nesting box on a wall sheltered from prevailing winds.

The Common Earthworm

UNDERGROUND

In damp weather, in the garden, one dig with a spade brings up several reddish-pink worms, each rarely more than twenty centimetres long. They quickly burrow underground again, but it is always possible to catch one.

The skin of the earthworm is moist, bare and slimy. This enables the worm to slither easily in the soil. It is through the skin that the worm breathes – it has no lungs. If an earthworm is placed in a dry spot or in the sun, its skin shrivels and it dies.

The body of the earthworm is divided into ring-like segments. These are clearly visible and easy to count. The animal has no skeleton. Each body segment has a circular muscle and can become either tight and narrow or loose and wide. These muscles and others running the length of the worm, enable it to crawl. Its underside has small bristles, the setae, which the worm can push into the soil when it moves or when a bird tries to pull it out of its burrow.

A common belief is that if a worm is cut in half it will grow into two worms. This is untrue and is not how the animal multiplies. In fact it will only survive if a small piece has been cut off.

Earthworms are hermaphrodite: they have both male and female organs. They exchange male sex cells – sperm – while they are united in pairs and all lay eggs from which hatch small, two-centimetre-long, worms.

TILLERS OF THE SOIL

The earthworm is an amazing help to the gardener as it improves the soil in which it lives. By digging burrows that sometimes go down several metres deep under the surface, the worm helps make the land better adapted for growing plants. The soil is aerated and rainwater can penetrate it easily.

Everyday the worm swallows huge quantities of earth: thirty times its weight when it is young, ten times when it is fully grown. Some is digested. The rest is rejected, but not before the worm's gastric juices have transformed it into a finer, more fertile soil. The chemicals in that soil are more easily absorbed by the roots of plants. The small coiled heaps of earth that you find on the ground in the garden, on the lawn, or on the path, are the earthworm's casts. So the worm churns the soil or in a way, ploughs it. Assisted by the mole, among others, it brings some materials to the soil surface or takes them down into the depth. This churning of the earth sometimes has dangerous consequences. In the 19th century, in France, sheep eating the grass of certain fields surprisingly died of the disease anthrax. One day, the scientist Louis Pasteur discovered that sheep that had died of anthrax had been buried in those fields years before. Earthworms had brought the deadly anthrax germs back to the soil surface in their casts. No one had, as some people believed, 'cast a spell' on the sheep.

IN LARGE NUMBERS

If there was only one earthworm, its action on the soil would be negligible. But earthworms are very numerous: in just one hectare of garden soil one can

The wormery.

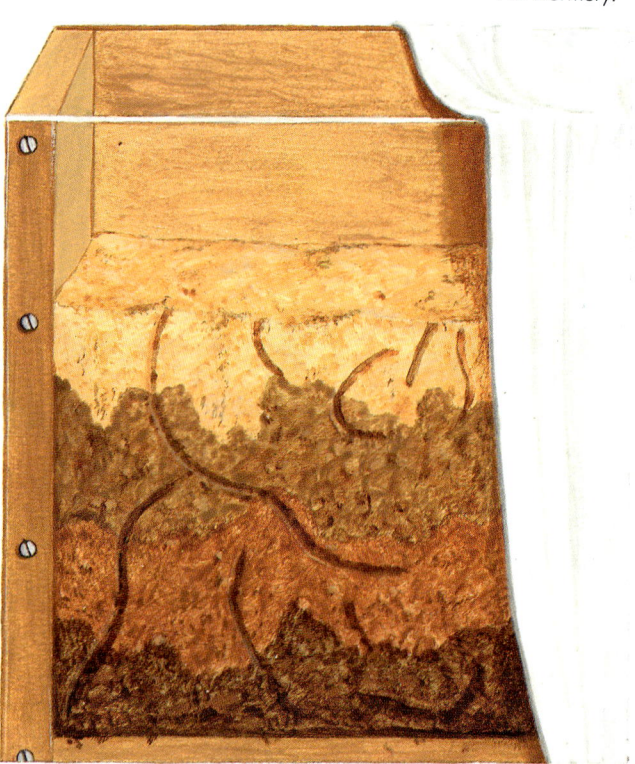

24

You can feel the bristles (setae) by gently caressing the earthworm's underside.

Male and female at the same time, the worms mate and then separate to lay their own eggs.

find between 350 and 1000 kilograms of worms. Imagine how many worms this represents!

When the ground is wet, after it has rained or you have watered the garden, take a torch and, after dark, go hunting for worms.

On the damp ground you will see dozens of worms – small ones, medium ones, big ones.

They will be partly hidden in their burrows, ready to disappear and escape you. The contraction of their segments and the grip of the bristles on their undersides against the walls of the burrows give them speed and strength when they move.

A WORMERY

You can study the way in which earthworms churn up the soil by building a wormery. This is a narrow little cage with clear glass or perspex walls. Fill it, in horizontal layers, with several kinds of soils of different colours. Cover the soil surface with a few dead leaves and dampen the soil well. Place a dozen worms in the cage then cover it with a black cloth and put it in the cellar or in a dark corner of the garden shed.

Every day, through the glass, you can record with tracing paper and coloured pencils the way in which the various soils have been mixed and study how the worms work underground.

Industry has managed to take advantage of the tireless activity of earthworms. In the last few years certain species of worm have been bred to process organic waste and fertilize soils. Enormous quantities of the worms are placed in large vats of earth and the waste added.

The Seven-Spot Ladybird

BEAUTIFUL BUT GREEDY

The red and black 'shell' of this ladybird is composed of two parts: the elytra, or wing cases, and the flying wings. The elytra can open and serve as protection for the two wings, which are transparent and fragile small membranes that are folded back when the ladybird is not flying.

At the end of the insect's legs, a system of hooks enables it to move along twigs, blades of grass and leaves.

The ladybird's shell has another role: its colour is a danger signal to any creatures that want to eat it, birds in particular. When the ladybird is threatened, it produces a drop of fluid that has a bitter taste and a very unpleasant smell.

The amazing 'jaws' of this small insect make it a formidable carnivore. Woe betide the aphids that get in its way – few will survive.

Ladybirds, like most other insects lay their eggs in batches. Each batch numbers from five to fifty eggs and is hidden under a leaf or tree bark. Each female will lay several batches.

About eight days after the eggs have been laid, blackish larvae come out of the egg cases.

They are as voracious as the adult ladybirds. However, they do not look at all like the parents. Like all insect larvae, they have to go through a series of changes, or metamorphosis, before becoming the insects that we know.

When about a month old, the larvae wrap themselves in an envelope for a few days to go through the last changes that will finally turn them into adult ladybirds. The adult's life lasts a little more than a year.

THE BEETLE OF OUR LADY

The name ladybird dates from the Middle Ages, when the beetles were associated with the Virgin Mary and called 'beetles of Our Lady'. Everyone has played with a ladybird, letting it run from one hand to the other then to the end of a finger until it flies off, or has counted the spots on its back as years of its life.

Of course, there is no truth in the idea of one spot, one year. In reality, ladybirds do not all have the same number of spots on their back and are not all the same colour because they belong to different species. There are, in fact, about 2 500 species of ladybird. There are ladybirds with 10, 14, 19, 20, 22, and even 24 spots. The most common ones are the seven-spot and two-spot ladybirds, which are red with black spots, sometimes black with red spots, and more rarely black, with yellow spots.

Even among these, the size and pattern of the spots may vary from one individual to another. If you make a little sketch of each one you see, you will remember them better and be able to compare them. You will realize that nature does not leave things to chance.

A VORACIOUS INSECT

There is nothing frightening about the ladybird. It is small, rounded, smooth, it does not sting, and it can be caught and admired easily. This is in contrast to, say, the grasshopper, the wasp, the fly or the mosquito, but also to the ladybirds' cousins, the beetles, which are not as prettily clothed.

Aphids must have a totally different opinion of the ladybird. To them it is a

The ladybird lays eggs in batches of 5 to 50.

The larva of the ladybird is very different from the adult insect.

(1) 22-spot ladybird.   (2) 5-spot ladybird.

Let us play with the ladybird. What will the weather be like tomorrow? If it flies away, the weather will be fine, they say.

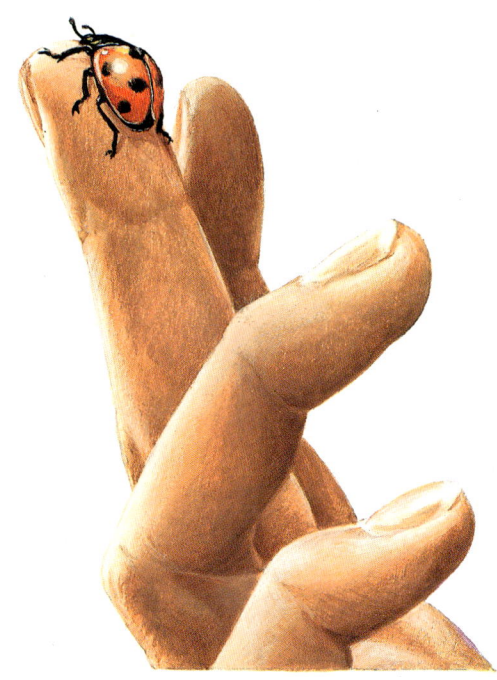

carnivore, or meat-eater, and a devourer of aphids. If you want to see this for yourself, put your ladybird on a branch covered with aphids and watch! It moves forward, cleaning up as it goes. No aphid escapes it – a real massacre. The ladybird is so voracious that it is used to combat insects that feed on and damage crops. In California, in the 1870s, ladybirds were used for the first time to destroy cottony-cushion scale insects, which attack orange groves.

A SWARM OF LADYBIRDS

Ladybirds hold another surprise for us. Did you know that they gather in their hundreds, or sometimes thousands, to spend the winter together. These gatherings are influenced by the number of hours of daylight and by temperature. In high places – on mountains, atop church steeples, for example – the ladybirds settle, year after year, in the same place. They remain huddled together over the winter months until it is time for each one to go away and resume its solitary life for the rest of the year.

A LARGE FAMILY

The ladybird has many cousins that, like itself, belong to the Coleoptera or beetle order of insects. Coleoptera all have elytra, the hard wing cases, sometimes brightly coloured, protecting their flying wings. Some live in water, such as the water-devil and the diving-beetle. Among the others, a few cause great damage to plants – for example the cockchafer, the weevil and the bark-beetle. Carabid beetles, like ladybirds, consume large quantities of insects harmful to vegetation.

The House Martin

A FAITHFUL NEIGHBOUR

Smaller than its close relative the swallow, the house martin is easily identified by its white rump patch that contrasts with the dark colour of its wings, tail and back.

In comparison with the swallow, its tail is less deeply forked and does not have the two long feathers that create a v-shape at the end. Its flight is fast and twisting. Seen from below, the house martin looks very white.

The house martin lives in villages and town, making its home under the eaves of houses or under balconies. It is becoming more and more unusual to find its nests in large groups.

When it arrives, the house martin gets busy building a nest that will be a home to one or two broods of four or five chicks. The adults must make haste as the young will have to be able to fly off to Africa by September.

During the few months that it spends in our towns, the house martin builds its nest and rears its young right under our eyes. It positions its nest against our houses, high enough above the ground so as to be out of reach. This location gives the martin almost total security.

A NEST WORTHY OF A MASON

As soon as it settles in an area, the bird chooses a suitable place to build the nest – on a wall or under a window ledge or roof.

To make its nest, it sticks together small pellets of earth. When martins are nest-building, they can be seen, sometimes dozens of them together, landing on the ground to collect the earth. The earth is powdery when dry, but once mixed with the bird's saliva it makes excellent mortar.

Do the martins choose their nest material? There is no doubt that they do as there are some soils they will never use. They rapidly build up the nest into a cup shape with a small oval entrance hole at the top.

If they build their nest near your home, you may be able to observe their construction work and perhaps count how many days it takes them to complete the job.

FAMILY LIFE

When the nest is finished, the male and female line the inside with a few blades of grass and, above all, lots of feathers. The female then starts to lay the eggs. She usually lays four or five and incubates them for fifteen days, occasionally helped by the male.

Once the chicks have hatched, they are constantly fed on regurgitated insects by both parents. The food is sometimes so plentiful that it overflows from the beak of the parent bird, giving the impression the martin has a moustache!

To get a better idea of the quantity of insects consumed, from a vantage point near the nest you can count how many feeding trips the parents make. And do not forget that these trips are made continuously from sunrise to sunset.

But also remember that, being an avid eater of insects, the house martin must be protected. Watching a nest too closely can disturb the feeding routine of the young. If the adult, arriving to feed its chicks, has to wait too long to give over its ball of insects, it will swallow it, depriving the young of a good meal. You must therefore be discreet and

The house martin's chicks are born blind and covered with fine down.

32

On the telegraph wires the house martin (1) and the swallow (2) are sometimes found side-by-side.

position yourself far enough from the nest so as not to disturb the birds. You then need to use binoculars to study them.

House martins produce two or sometimes even three broods each year. The young birds from the first brood help feed their younger brothers and sisters. They all squeeze into the nest at night to roost and some nests end up housing about ten birds. The record is thirteen roosting in one nest.

A TIRELESS TRAVELLER

In September, migration starts. The whole population of martins flies off to Africa, travelling, weather permitting, for six to eight hours a day at a cruising speed of thirty to forty kilometres an hour. If the dryness of the Sahara desert does not decimate them or African birds of prey feed on them, you might see your house martins again, in the same colony, next year.

MESSENGER OF SPRING

Popular wisdom says that swallows and house martins are a sign that spring is coming. Swallows arrive first, house martins about two weeks after. To check this, make a note, every year, of the date when the first swallows appear. In general, this takes place at the end of March or the beginning of April. Is the following period mild and do fine-weather days become more frequent?

People also say that one swallow does not make a summer. What should we believe? Indeed, it is wise not to rejoice too soon on seeing just one swallow. We should wait for more to arrive for confirmation of improving weather conditions!

The Mole

MOUNDS ON THE LAWN

The presence of a mole in the garden does not go unnoticed: molehills multiply. But it is actually rather difficult to see the animal. However, you might one day be fortunate enough to find one that a cat has captured and brought to the doorstep.

The mole's dark grey, almost black, fur is short and dense. Its barrel-shaped body continues in a flattened head without a distinct neck. Hidden in the fur on its head, its eyes and flapless ears are invisible. Its pink snout is almost hairless. It has very short limbs ending with five-toed broad paws. The front paws are much stronger than the hind ones. The mole uses its front paws as shovels to dig its tunnels.

The mole organizes its underground territory to suit its needs for shelter, hunting and rearing of its young. It makes the central nesting cavity, lined with grass and twigs, into a true underground fortress with a network of tunnels round it. Some tunnels, usually circular in shape, are for ventilation, while the rest, which are longer and straighter, serve as hunting grounds.

The jaws of the mole bear cutting incisor teeth, sharp canines and pointed molars that enable it to kill its prey. It cannot easily see the animals on which it feeds; sound and smell, rather than sight, inform it of its prey's nature – mostly earthworms and insect larvae and adults. It eats at least half its bodyweight in food every day.

The mole sometimes ventures out of its tunnels to hunt for small garden animals above ground.
It burrows back underground at the slightest sign of danger.

The mole hunts within a complicated network of tunnels.

EQUIPPED FOR UNDERGROUND WORK

If the mole takes a fancy to the soil in your garden you will soon see molehills appear. Often, the nest will be situated under the largest one. To shovel and move such quantities of soil and make these hills, what tools does this furry miner use?

Every part of the mole's body shows that it is a very efficient burrowing animal. Each nostril is protected by a fold of skin that prevents earth from getting into it. Each toe is armed with a flat, sharp, cutting claw. Its short hair does not have a set, or fixed direction of growth, and so allows the animal to go forwards or backwards without problems. The mole moves easily along its network of tunnels and can reach a speed of one metre a second.

One might think that an animal which lives underground would be dirty and covered in dust. On the contrary, the mole's dense fur provides a protective coat against particles of soil.

A DESTROYER OF LARVAE

With the help of its shovel-like paws used in a swimming motion, the mole excavates the soil. throwing earth out sideways or backwards to form molehills. It can dig tunnels at a rate of a few dozen metres a day.

The mole plays a part in aerating the ground in which it digs its network of tunnels. These 'earthworks' allow a thorough churning of the particles and chemicals that compose arable land. The earth of a molehill is fine in texture and light to the touch as if it had been seived by a patient gardener.

In the garden, the mole performs another service. Always hungry, the animal automatically destroys all the larvae it comes across, most of which attack cultivated plants.

NEIGHBOURS' SQUABBLES

Gardeners and moles do not get on well, however. The gardener does not like finding the mole's 'castles' in the vegetable patch or in the middle of the lawn. Also, the mole is not easy to get rid of. It is even more difficult to catch than it is to see.

It is said that the moles does not like draughts around its 'fortress' and that if you open one of its tunnels, there is a fair chance it will come and repair the damage.

You can try to make it go away by planting flowers such as some fritillaries around the molehills. However, acknowledging that the mole can be of service, some gardeners, who are more amenable, put up with its excavations in the garden.

THE MOLE-CATCHER

In the past, the mole-catcher would be called to get rid of these generally undesirable mammals. Part wizard, part hunter, this strange, slightly frightening person, went about laden with traps, and peddled his services from farm to farm. The catcher used to skin the moles caught in the traps and sell the pelts for the making of much sought-after garments such as jackets and coats. To make a single coat, 2500 pelts were required!

The mole's young are born in the central tunnel.

The Garden Spider

A TRAP SET IN THE GARDEN

How can one explain the repulsion some of us feel towards spiders? Those spiders that live in our gardens are indeed quite harmless and display a wealth of patience and ingenuity. One of them, the European garden spider, is the most remarkable as much by virtue of the elegance of its shape and colours as by the magnificence of its web.

The European garden spider captures its prey in its orb web, a true circular trap of fine silken threads produced by glands in its abdomen.

A liquid substance is secreted by these glands and comes out through the spinnerets situated near the tip of the abdomen, hardening on contact with the air while still remaining supple. Whatever insect gets caught in the web – fly, mosquito, bee – the spider eats.

The sensitive hairs on its eight legs are permanently in contact with the web and tell the animal about its catch. It quickly injects the victim with a poison that paralyses but does not kill the prey, which the spider then devours at its leisure. From its salivary glands, and through its pincer-like mouth parts, the spider pours digestive juices into the insect's body in order to liquefy its contents. It then sucks up the liquid meal.

The spider family is fascinating because of its diversity. Some spiders are microscopic. Others, mostly in tropical countries, are as large as your hand and are highly poisonous. A few live underground, others in water. There are some that can cross oceans, carried along by the wind. Certain spiders can spin silken threads thirty metres or more in length, which is over

1000 times their own size!

Among the Arachnida, which differ from insects by bearing four, not three, pairs of walking legs, are classified animal as diverse as harvestmen, scorpions, ticks and the 30000 species of spider.

THE SPINNER WAS TOO CLEVER

An old legend says that Arachne, a young Greek girl, was excellent at spinning and weaving. She was such an expert that she boasted she was better than the goddess Athena, the Spinner of the Gods.

The goddess took up the challenge. Arachne, however, produced such perfect material that Athena could find no fault with it. Furious, Athena tore up her rival's work and struck the girl. Frightened by this, Arachne, in the same way spiders dangle at the end of a thread, hanged herself with a rope. Taking pity on her, Athena brought Arachne back to life but in the shape of a spider. It is from this story of the unfortunate Arachne that spiders were given the scientific name of Arachnida.

A MASTERPIECE OF WEAVING

In our gardens, the European garden spider is common and easy to observe. Is it as beautiful as Arachne was long ago? Look at it, motionless in the centre of its web, head downwards, legs held together in pairs. If you are careful not to touch the web you will be able to admire the animal at your leisure. A magnifying glass will prove useful for a closer, more detailed look. Make a sketch of the patterns on the spider's abdomen and legs. The white spots on its back, resembling the diamonds of a

By temporarily keeping a diadem spider prisoner, you can force it to work while you watch it.

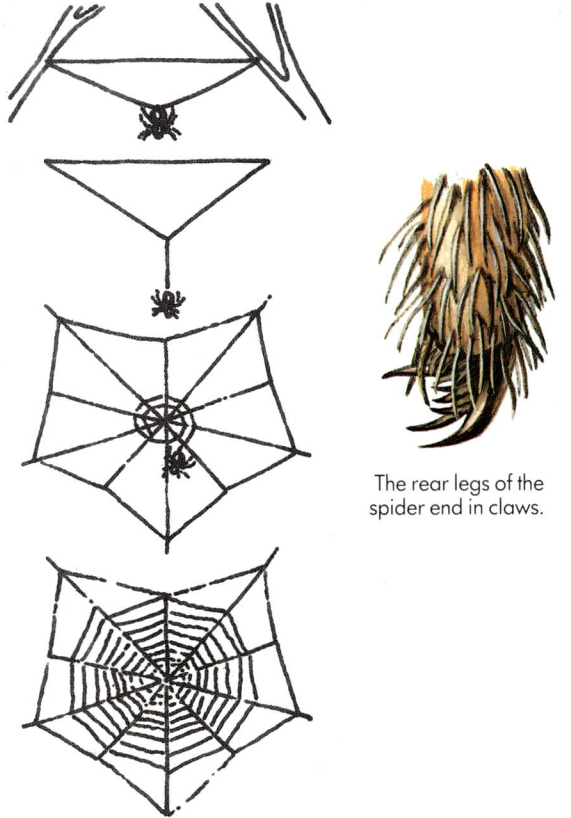

The rear legs of the spider end in claws.

The various stages in the spinning of the web.

crown, explain its other popular name of diadem spider.

Is it also a skilful weaver? Admire its web, a perfect piece of work, on a crisp morning when the dewdrop-laden threads shimmer in the light of the rising sun. This masterpiece is so fine, so harmonious, that many photographers have been tempted to capture it on film. Try this for yourself. The result is often unexpected, sometimes quite beautiful.

When the cartwheel-shaped web is complete the spider retires to a hiding place, perhaps under a leaf, and waits.

HOW DOES THE TRAP WORK?

While you are looking at the web, try to understand why it is made in such a way and what is its purpose.

To find out how the insect-trap works, you must catch a fly, taking great care not to kill it, and place it gently on the web. What happens then? Look how the spider sets about paralysing the prey and how the fly tries to free itself in a last flutter of wings. When the struggle is all over, try to take the fly back. Is it possible to free it from the silken cocoon in which it is trapped? Is it still alive?

Repeat the experiment with another fly and then, by gently shaking a corner of the web with a small twig, see how many times the spider is deceived into believing other insects have become trapped. What happens if you blow on the web as the wind does?

With the twig, gently tear one or two threads. How does the spider react? When and how does it repair the web? How long does this mending take?

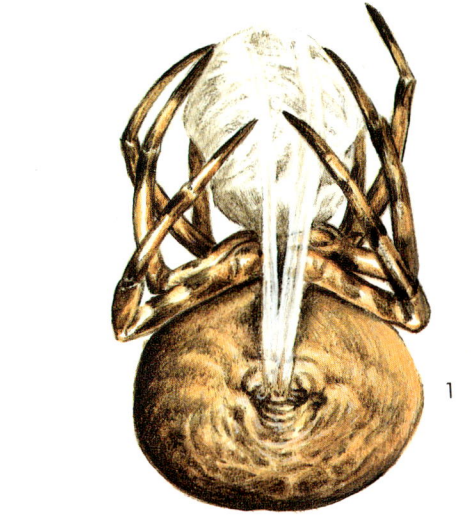

1

2   3

From the abdomen a thick liquid comes out that dries on contact with the air and produces the silk strands (1).

the female (2) and the male (3).

The Cat

A DOMESTIC FELINE

We have turned the cat into a companion of our sedentary life and seem to have forgotten that it belongs to the same animal family as the tiger and the panther.

The cat's gait is supple and silent. With its long back legs and powerful muscles it can jump high and far. When it runs, its top speed can reach forty kilometres an hour.

Its claws enable it to cling firmly to tree trunks and branches and to get out of apparently dangerous situations even when it is only a kitten.

Its sharp hearing, keen sense of smell and piercing eyesight allow it to stalk its prey, even at night. It pounces on the animal or chases it. With its sharp claws, the cat pins it down to the ground. Its teeth, especially the four dagger-like canines, enable it to kill its prey quickly. Then, if it is hungry, it devours its victim, but sometimes it abandons it after spending a long time playing with it, or comes to drop it at your feet as an offering.

AN ALOOF COMPANION

In the house, the cat spends long periods lying still and quiet. It likes warmth and company, but it often walks off proudly, shunning caresses and showing contempt as you try and stroke it with your hand. In this manner, the cat shows the limits of its dependence on us. It can also, more easily than a dog, be left alone in the house should its owner have to go out for a short time. It is fond of its own living area and does not like to change its habits.

A DEMANDING PRESENT

At the age of two months, a kitten can be taken away from its mother. Provided you train it, the kitten soon learns to keep clean without her help. It suckles its mother's milk because it enjoys it rather than needs it, and it gradually develops a taste for food more suited to its carnivorous nature: when the kitten has started to eat meat, that is the time you can adopt it. But beware, the little kitten, so soft to stroke, so funny to watch, will grow into a cat and, above all, will need you every day. When adult, the cat is no longer especially amusing.

The cat is an animal which, in spite of its ability to hunt, can be kept indoors. It keeps its owner company, who, in return, is at its service. This involves preparing its meals, keeping its mess-tray clean, providing something to 'do its claws' on and convincing the neighbour to look after it while the owner is away on holiday. But also, the owner must spend time proving to the cat by gestures and by voice – a cat is very sensitive to the human voice – that it is a friend. So many demands on the person who undertook, one day, to live with a cat!

A THREATENED HUNTER

One day Puss disappears. What has happened to it? Has it gone hunting? Some cats have been known to disappear from home for six months at a time and then return from nearby woods with its original coat transformed into the fawn-coloured coat of a wild cat. But perhaps it is pursuing a female cat 'on heat', that is a she-cat ready to mate and become pregnant? Or maybe

When it feels its young are in danger, the mother carries them in its mouth to a safe place.

it is locked in the garage or shed or has fallen wherever its curiosity took it? Is it caught in a bush by its loose flea-collar? Is it hurt and hiding until it is better? One day it may return with a badly injured leg or with lead pellets in its back. Traps and guns are a threat to the cat that looks for food in the woods.

If Puss gets lost far from home, it becomes a feral or wild cat and as such is in danger. The cat that covers 600 kilometres to find its home has an exceptional sense of direction or amazing luck.

A BONUS OF KITTENS

Living with a she-cat means accepting the responsibility of welcoming kittens into the house. Several times a year, female cats are on heat. Unless you want kittens, keep your she-cat indoors during these occasions. If you allow it to go out, its miaowing, particularly at night, will soon attract the neighbourhood tom-cats.

Two months later, the she-cat will give birth to three, four, or perhaps five kittens. If it hides them at the bottom of the wardrobe or in the linen basket, you will have no trouble finding them. But you might see the cat come back, after several days' absence, slim and agile again. You must follow it cautiously to learn where it has left its litter.

There are five kittens. They are already alert and lively. What will you do with them? Can you keep them? Will you have to have them put down?

Fortunately, timely precautions such as cat birth pills, hormone injections or a sterilization operation, avoid too great a number of births. This way you will not experience hearing your female cat crying for its lost young.

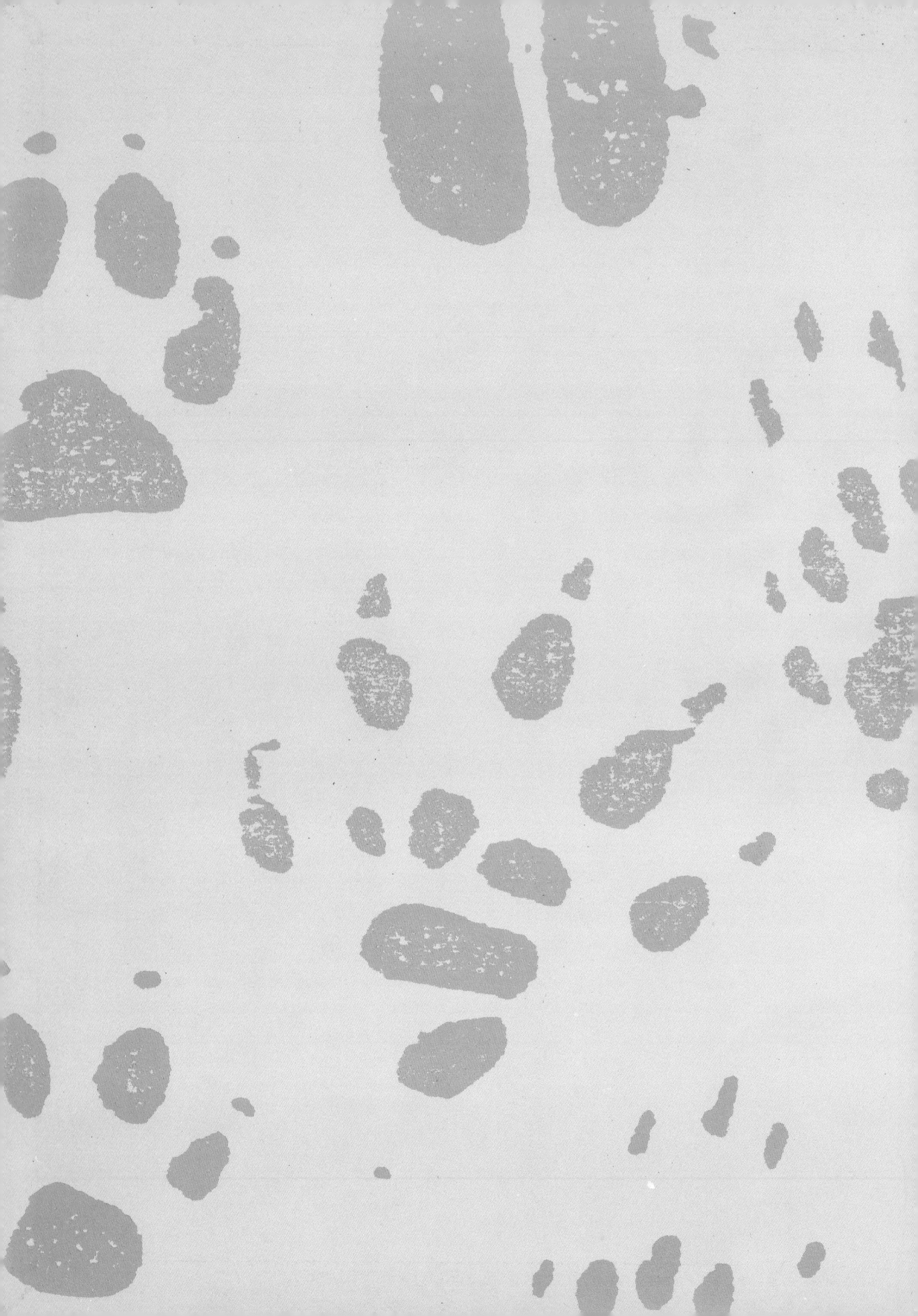